Life's Loving

A Book of Poems About How Life Loved Me Into Being

Emily Perkins

Made with ❤ on the BookLeaf Publishing Platform

www.bookleafpub.in

www.bookleafpub.com

Dedication

To my women. My sisters. You are my sanctuary and my remedy.

Acknowledgements

Thank you to my partner, my love. Daniel, you are my heart's deepest desire made manifest. Thank you for loving the versions of me that came before you, the ones that were birthed alongside you, and for choosing the many more me's to come. I love our magic.

Thank you to all of my teachers and mentors for the warm reflections, the powerful reflections, the reflections that shatter the illusions and help me see myself better. You are the spark that lights the torches, illuminating the way as I venture towards the calling of my soul. I am so very grateful for your wisdom and guidance.

And to you my darling Obsidian, my baby boy. Thank you for choosing me as your mama and for birthing the version of me I am most excited to be. I love you, sweet boy.

Preface

Life's Loving is a compilation of heart songs. The words that were the medicine that came in the hard moments, the moments of reverence and the moments of awe and awareness. It is a journey of years of becoming through the grace of how Life loved me and in turn, taught me to love myself.

Treasure Hunting

I love buried treasure.
I love venturing into the depths to unearth
what has been hidden.
The rusty, jagged trinkets left in the shadowy
places.
The ones shrouded in shame or rage or
loneliness.
Glasses thick like clay
that have kept life small.
I love shining the flashlight of my love into
the thicket
where they got left
after society or hurt made them bury
themselves.
These hidden and forgotten
treasures inside
are the key to my restoration.
Wiping off the dirt and smut
so it can feel seen and beautiful
again,
and then bringing it back home
to the sanctuary of my love.

Seeds

I have been using a packet of wildflower seeds
as a bookmark.
It feels appropriate.
Seeds are the beginnings,
before the roots.
Tucked into pages of the books I read most.
Made of Rivers by Emory Hall
Why I Wake Early by Mary Oliver
Rhythms and Roads by Victoria Erickson
The Sun and Her Flowers by Rupi Kaur
Women whose brilliance ignites and soothes.
The friends that sat by my bedside, ready and
available in the gone moments.
Their souls seem to know my own.
Their words, the seeds planted in my heart
to now bloom into becoming the thing I have
long adored.
~ Women Poets

Body Stories

Tell me the story of your body.
The moments, the marks and the mumblings
that become the words etched into your flesh.
Tell me of your liberation.
The sloughing off of the dead skin,
the shaking and loosening of the script
you were never meant to follow.

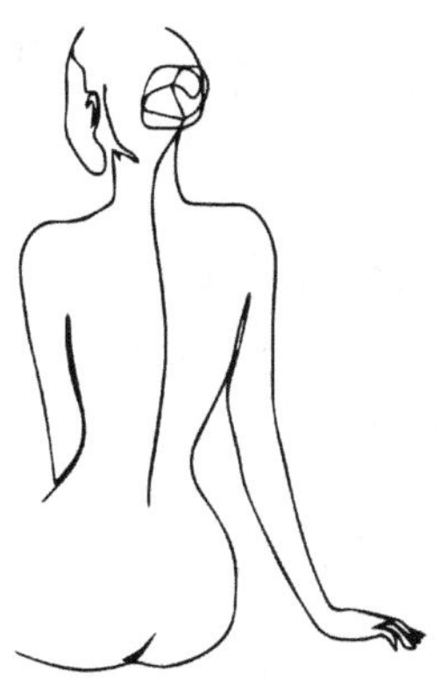

How Do You Love Yourself?

How do you love yourself?
Like a dear friend.
A confident, loyal, trustworthy, honest and
kind.
Like a lover.
Fierce, passionate, tender, devoted, giving and
loving.
Like a parent.
A safe haven, nurturing, supportive,
protective and wise.
This is how you love yourself.
To be the friend, the lover, the mother and
the father to yourself
that you have always needed.

Kneading to Bind

Where the light pours in,
my eyes catch the dance of fairy dust in the
beam of summer sun.
A wetness in the air kisses my lips good
morning.
Appreciation for this simple magic
reaches from the tips of my toes to the ends
of my hair.
My life... my... life.
Sprinkled with layers of ingredients.
The meat of my heart pulverized
to release the juices and the flavor.
The dough of my body, kneaded to bind the
ingredients.
Tenderized, full-bodied, whole.

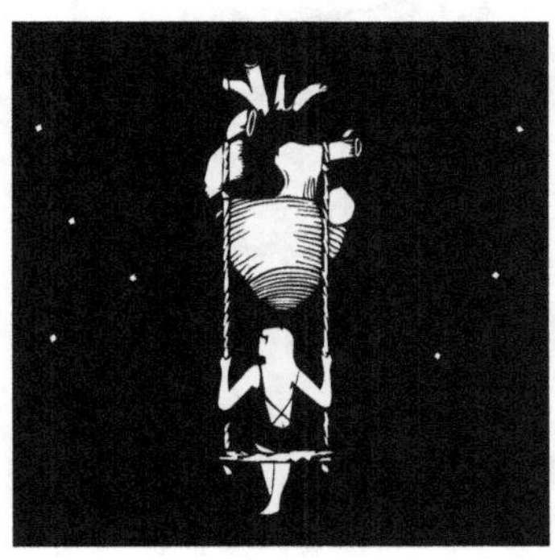

Siren Call

I want to be cherished like a goddess.
Not because I am special,
which I am.
Not because I am a woman,
which is reason enough.
But because it is the kind of love I give
and I deserve what I give.

Vulnerability

If you want deep love
you can not live on the surface of it.

Waters

Water pulling, pushing, sucking and swirling.
70 percent of me.
The thing I need to live,
the current of my feeling,
the sway of the feminine.
I feel you moving me.
I feel you.
The subtle yet powerful transformation of the
waters that are shaping me.
Rearranging my cells to a new way, a new
human, a new woman.
Birthing yet again in the darkness of the deep
waters.
Swimming to the surface for air,
to let the beams of sun warm and soften my
face.
Taking a breath
before the current grabs my feet,
taking me to a new depth.
There are moments I am swimming with the
current of life,

some I am riding the wave with strength and
finesse,
and sometimes the waves are rolling and
dragging me down.
This watery existence is somehow stretching
me.
Asking me to hold more.
More life
more pain
more pleasure
more love
more trust
more loss
more grief
more responsibility
more of myself and less of myself.
After so much swimming
my body is begging me to float.
To surrender to the current
and let it gently take me down the river.
To trust that I don't have to fight, force, or
figure out.
There is such relief in the mystery.
In the becoming, inside of the unknown.
Let the feelings come and pass through.

Let the mind, in its efforts to know,
know what it can and leave the rest.
Let the body bring me home
again and again.
The shadows are not meant to be hiding
places but quiet corners to reflect,
and then open the window to let the breeze
in.

Grief

You live in my love.
In the mist of the sea and my salty tears.
You live in the swell.
Ocean tides rise and crash with waves of
emotion.
A heart can only break if love lived there.
You live in my love.

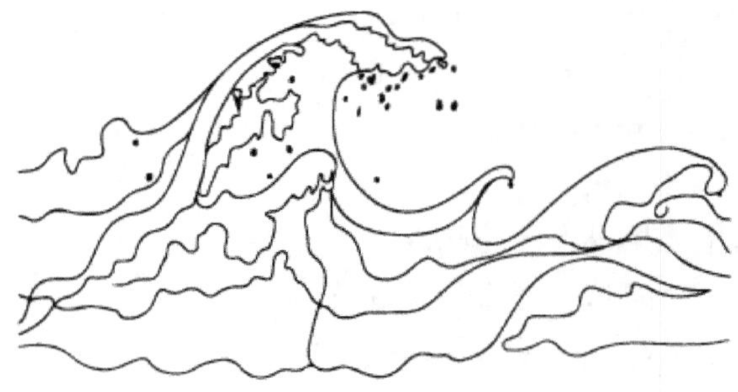

Holy Breaking

When Life takes you,
when the breaking happens
you wonder,
how could I have not seen this coming?
Well darling,
you aren't meant to know everything.
There is no escaping the mess of Life.
She will take you where you need to go,
not necessarily where you envisioned.
Rage, judgement, fire, cages my heart and
stifles my light.
Real, present, necessary.
Cyclical cycles of divine doing.
Starting to bleed on the day I was meant to
give birth.
Thunderous cracking as I find out my worst
fear has been made manifest
one year from its ignition into my system.
The phoenix fire blazes and smells of pine and
power.
The holy breaking that has created this
masterpiece of a body and being.
I see your, our, brilliant work in every line,

every fissure mended with gold
or maybe the whole of me is gold.
Not mended, but gold completely,
exposed by the earthquake.

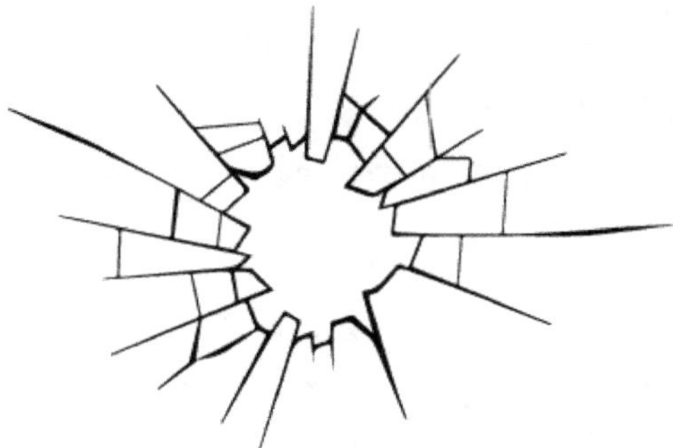

The Medicine

Meet others
with a warm heart.
Regardless of our storylines,
we all require the same medicine.
Care.
Judgement is the dull knife
that slowly severs
the thing we all long for most.
Connection.
The illusion, thick glasses
that project a fiction that we are separate.

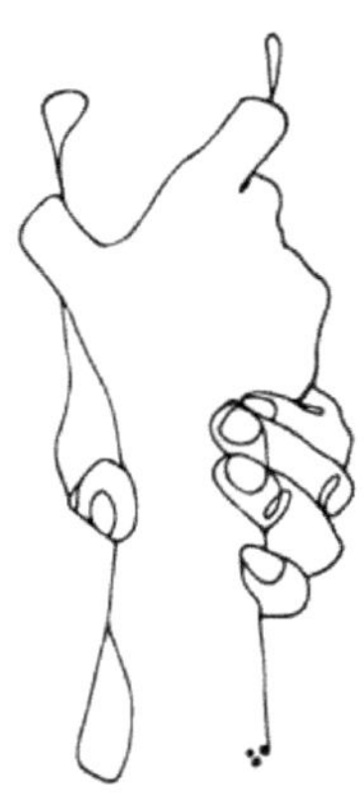

The Magic of You

If I ever question magic,
I think of you.
The man who matches me.
The divine timing of our parallel lines
merging.
Our shared stories and scars.
Our shared ways of seeing and loving.
It could only be you.
As soon as we began
my body wanted no one else.
And when our bones were broken by our own
shadows, we mended back stronger.
Continually struck with awe and wonder
by the man you choose to be.
A devotion to all that matters with a steadfast
ease.
I choose this life with
you, my precious gift.
I choose our love to
uplift.

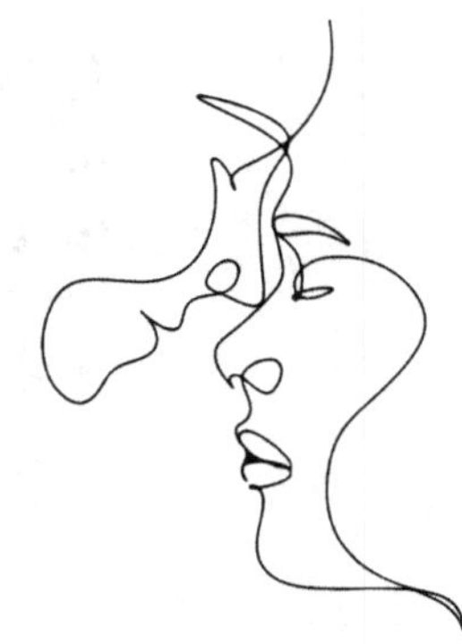

Breath

I drink in this delicious elixir
watch as my chest rises and expands with life.
Falls and sets free what's not needed.
Breathe deep and life feels full and possible.
Shallow feels heavy and hard.
My built-in reset button.
Breathe
and I begin again.
Breathe
and I choose.
A life that is mine, expansive and alive
or tight and short, controlled by
circumstance.

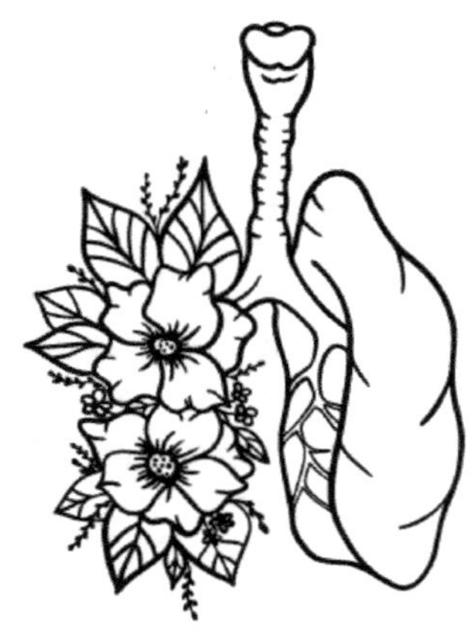

Birth

Resilience took on a new meaning
in the portal of birth.
Breathing, bouncing, swaying
with every contraction
with the trust that the pain had a purpose.
Waiting for the expansion and opening as
reward,
only to find out that I was where I had
started.
Days pass and I am still here.
Still trusting, somehow, that I can.
As soon as you emerge,
the how, our arduous journey, vanishes in the
feel of your skin against mine.
Where doubt lived,
now there is an embodied knowing
that I can do anything.

A New World

December 3rd 2023
The birthing of three new lives.
One new to the earthly plane and
two new to a world we have never known
before.
Parenthood
In a moment, everything changes
and we are birthed, catapulted
ready or not
into love, into a growing-up
of all three of us.
Together, fumbling forward, hand in hand
Into this new world.
Adventure awaits!

Feeding You

Tiny feather-light fingers
float across my skin.
The softest fairy kisses
blessing my arms
my chest
my face.
My favorite feeling in the world.
I only now know.
This is bliss.

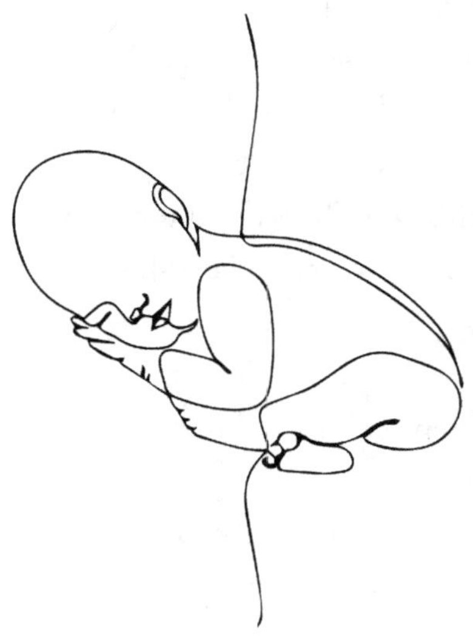

Shame

I've been visiting the older versions of myself
that I am embarrassed of.
They have been tucked away in a closet,
dusty and smelling of longing.
The me's that allowed men into my body
for attention, a moment of perceived love, for
power.
The me's that did not know what I know now.
I thought I knew, which makes the shame that
much sharper.
Shame has a way of dominating a story.
It lies heavy in the body.
A sinking in the solar plexus.
All of a sudden I become a moment.
When the truth is rarely singular,
but rather a multicolored tapestry.
Self-aware, loving, powerful, strong,
and
still learning the strategies,
the golden masks over the
shadows.
Come here shadows, let me
hold you for a while.

Home

The sweet nectar
of my own love
softly lands me back home.

Women

We are the womb of the world,
the creators of life.
Our sisterhood is balm for the burns.
Our self-liberation is the stuff of miracles.
We walk into this future
with our heads high
our hearts open
and our hands clasped together.

Pleasures

Mmmm.
A playful breeze tickles my skin.
The sweet, full-bodied floral of lilies
feels like it fills my veins with sunshine.
Every inch of me feeling its beauty.
Cashmere hugs my body in a warm and
tender embrace.
The reverberation of a song that makes life
come to life.
Cells open and vibrating with feeling
and I bask in its tonic.
The way a fresh pastry makes me pause,
take a breath and revel in its deliciousness.
The way your fingers gently weave into the
hair draped on the back of my neck.
Presence makes pleasures possible.
Pleasures give way to the yummiest ingredient
of all.
The one that connects the dots
from moments to meaning.
Gratitude.
Deep abiding gratitude.

For the breeze, the lilies, for cashmere's
embrace, the pastries, the adoring fingers and
the songs that crack me open and shake me
free.
I love you Life.

The All of It

Contraction and expansion,
contraction and expansion.
Life birthing me over and over.
Every version, nestled warmly
inside this russian doll.
Every version with its own
grimoire.
All welcome around the hearth of my heart.
Holding hands and sharing stories
of the pain that unleashed the power.
Oh, how I love this dance with Life.
This epic saga of challenge and bliss.
From the nagging pain in my hip to the
intoxicating smell of a lily.
A four-day labor,
to the feel of your tiny fingers.
I love the all of it.
Not either
Or.
Nothing rejected or cast
away.
The multicolored beauty
of the ALL.